HOW TO GET RICH FROM HOME ON A PART TIME BASIS WITH ONLY $20

START MAKING MONEY IN THE NEXT 48 HOURS

Christopher Mitchell

www.ChangeYourLifeOvernight.com

HOW TO GET RICH FROM HOME ON A PART TIME BASIS WITH ONLY $20! START MAKING MONEY IN THE NEXT 48 HOURS!

Copyright © 2017 Christopher Mitchell

ISBN-13: 978-1543088465

ISBN-10: 1543088465

Printed In The United States Of America.

TABLE OF CONTENTS:

The book you're about to read contains proven strategies that will help a person make money from home starting with only twenty dollars. The author shares valuable information in this book that he has used to do exactly what the title of this book states. If you want to get rich, you absolutely must own your own business. The author can teach you how to do this through this book, as well as his other books. If you want to speak to Christopher, or perhaps join his team and have him become your personal mentor, feel free to contact him at his website listed here. God bless you!

www.ChangeYourLifeOvernight.com

Introduction:

Testimonials

I LOVE this book! Christopher makes this straight forward and an easy read. It will motivate you and make you deal with your complacency and fears. All the excuses that often hinder us from doing what we desire to do Christopher covered in his book. It will encourage you to go forward and empower you with the easy 123 step approach and the exact tools needed to help you share what God has locked up inside of you to help somebody else! A wealth of information! **~Laura**

Christopher is amazing. This guy actually did what he promoted in his book. Take his advice! He knows what he's talking about. He practiced what he preached. He is very experienced and not just copying someone else's research. Christopher is the real deal. **~Michael**

This is an excellent plan and is easy to follow. Christopher writes in an easy to read, conversational style. The book is full of reasons why you should stop living in poverty and start living in abundance. I've followed his steps and I've seen awesome results in my life. It's easy to follow and I recommend it to everyone. **~Ricky**

Now there is no excuse to make your dreams come true. Can't wait to see my book come to life. Thanks a lot Christopher! **~Jeffrey**

This is a phenomenal book! Easy to read and simple to understand for you to unlock your dreams. I never thought it would be this easy! **~Vertis**

This is GOLD for anyone who has ever had a dream of wanting to become rich. As Christopher points out, everyone has goals and dreams in life, but most people never pursue them because of the lies and self-doubt that we allow to hinder us. Christopher makes getting rich EASY. You're not looking at the staircase, just the first step. And after that, the second step. I'm thrilled to discover that I really can accomplish what I thought was impossible. Thank you Christopher! I never in a million years would have thought it could be so simple! **~Donna**

Most people dream of getting rich when they're young, but as we get older we give up on our dreams just so we can pay the bills. I've lived with regret working at my dead end job for the last 30 years, but after reading Christopher's book on how to get rich on a part time basis I've got my joy and excitement back in life. It's people like Christopher who share their wisdom with the world that enables others like me to have a second chance in life. If I ever have the chance of meeting Christopher in person I'm taking him to the nicest restaurant I can find. Dinner is on me. **~Michelle**

I've owned my own business my entire life because it was handed down to me from my father. I wasn't passionate about the business, but felt I had to keep it going because it was in the family. After reading Christopher's book I realized how short life is to be doing something that you hate every single day. He inspired me to start all over and now I'm loving my life more than ever before. **~Tommy**

I never believed that I could make money from home until after I read Christopher's book. I was a little nervous, but followed his method step by step, exactly as he laid it out. I can't believe I made $2,100 n my first 30 days from only having worked about ten hours. That's half of my monthly salary at my job and I have to work two hundred hours to make that money. Believe me when I tell you, I'm going to be quitting my job very soon. My future is looking really good. **~Teresa**

Leaders are Readers, but we are also very careful who we let speak into our lives. That being said, my family and I have all of Christopher Mitchell's books. I recommend them all, especially this one. It takes money to live in this world and the rich people get to enjoy life much more than poor people. We owe it to ourselves to get rich. Great book Christopher! Thanks for being loyal and publishing it. **~Adrienne**

Christopher Mitchell is going to change a lot of people's lives with this book. This is an amazing book that needs to be shared with people all over the world. Awesome job Christopher! I bought your other book yesterday and I'm so excited to get rich. **~Robert**

I know Christopher Mitchell. He speaks the truth. He's a student of God's word. More than that, he lives it. What he's telling us to do in this book is how he lives his life. Get rich so you can bless others. This book will fire up your life! **~Eric**

Chapter One:

Who Am I?

My name is Christopher Mitchell. I was born on January 9th, 1979 in Houston, Texas. Two years later, my younger brother Andrew was born. My parents were complete opposites. My mom was an angel from Heaven. My dad, well, like I said, he was the opposite.

When I was three years old my dad cheated on my mom. My mom divorced my dad and became a single mother. She worked as a secretary at Ohio Wesleyan University in Delaware, Ohio. With a tiny salary, two young boys, food, clothes, a car, insurance, an apartment, as well as other expenses to pay for, as you can probably imagine, my mom struggled financially.

When I was seven years old I was sitting on the living room floor with my mom sitting behind me on the couch. I looked at her and said these exact words that I will NEVER forget for as long as I live:

Mom, I'm going to become rich someday, and when I do I'm going to take care of you and you're never going to have to struggle again. She looked me in the eyes, told me she believed me, and then started crying. Just two years later, when I was nine years old, my mom suddenly died from cancer. It took everyone by surprise. She was perfectly healthy one day and then out of nowhere she was gone. She was only thirty-five years old when she passed away.

It's been almost thirty years since my mom passed away, but I'm still holding on to life lessons that I learned from her. I was blessed to have the greatest mom in the world for nine years. She was the best! I'll never forget her. I look forward to the day when I get to see here again.

When my mom passed away my dad automatically regained custody of me and my brother. He had remarried and his wife had a daughter of her own. My dad also had a collection of cats and dogs that he couldn't properly care for. My brother and I were now living with my dad, his wife, her daughter, and a total of three cats and ten dogs.

It was a miserable living situation. My dad and his wife fought every single day without exception. My dad screamed every single time he opened his mouth. He was a terrible dad and a terrible husband. My brother and I stayed out of the house as much as we could because we feared being around our dad more than we feared The Devil. He was very hateful and abusive. My mom did nothing but love me and encourage me, while my dad did nothing but hate me and abuse me.

When I became a freshman in high school I joined the wrestling team and started working out. One day after I arrived home from wrestling practice my dad was in one of his usual rages. He started yelling at me to clean the house and I simply said no! Like always, he didn't like that, so he came toward me to beat me yet again, but this time something had changed. I had taken enough abuse from this man. I had gained a lot of size and strength from working out and something inside of me snapped! I had reached my breaking point! I defended myself against my dad.

Instead of him throwing me across the room, this time I picked him up and threw him across the room. After I threw him across the room I ran over to him, put him in a wrestling move, and completely popped both of his shoulders out of their sockets. His third wife at the time called 911 and the ambulance immediately rushed him to the emergency room. He stayed in the hospital for a few days because of the damage I had done to him physically. When he came home from the hospital he kicked me out of the house at that very moment.

I was now fifteen years old and unsure of where to go. I was only a freshman in high school. I didn't even have my driver's license yet, let alone a car to get around in. I made some phone calls and ended up moving in with a few relatives. I moved in with my grandparents for a while, then I moved in with an Aunt for a while, and then I moved in with an Uncle for a while. I bounced around back and forth between these relatives houses until I became an official adult.

When I turned eighteen years old I received a government check from my mom's death. That check allowed me to buy my first car and move into my own apartment. I still had five months until I graduated high school, but I was already living in my own apartment. At this point in my life I became a complete loner. I didn't hang out with people anymore. I was a health fanatic who ate healthy and took great care of my body, while all of my so-called high school friends either drank beer, or smoked pot every single day. I wasn't about to become another statistic who gave up on my goals and dreams in life just to become a loser. All I did was go to school, workout, and go to baseball practice. I hated school, but I had to attend in order to play baseball. Baseball was my life! I was good! Really good! My dream was to become a Major League Baseball Player. I had just one problem. I was small! Really small! That's why I started working out a few years earlier. I wanted to get bigger, faster, and stronger for baseball.

I went on to graduate high school just like everyone else, despite bouncing around for three years. I received a four year college scholarship for free from Ohio Wesleyan University in honor of my mom, but I knew college would never teach me how to become rich, so I told them to keep it. I passed on going to school and tried out for the big leagues instead. I went down to Lakeland, Florida to

The Detroit Tigers spring training camp. I was hoping my Major League Baseball career was about to kick off, but I started having all kinds of pain in my joints. To make a long story short, I ended up having five surgeries in the next sixteen months on both of my elbows, both of my shoulders, and my right knee. I never played baseball again.

When I finally admitted to myself that I was never going to play baseball again, I got depressed. I moved to Los Angeles, California and got totally beat up by life. I got involved in everything. I started a personal training business. I became a fitness model. I became a male stripper. I even became a male prostitute. I was so unhappy at one point that I drove to Malibu and almost committed suicide by jumping off a high cliff over-looking the ocean.

I've moved over 100 times in my lifetime. I've lived in nine different states, and I've been homeless in five of them. I've started over twenty-five businesses and failed in all of them.

I've been in a car crash where the paramedics had to cut my car to pieces with the jaws of life to get me out. I caught the woman who I was about to marry cheating on me. I've been evicted from my homes, I've had my cars repossessed, I've had my bank accounts overdrawn so many times I can't even keep track, and I've even had a jealous hater falsely accuse me of being a scam artist, a child rapist, a gay porn star, and a dangerous threat to society from all of the steroids that I take. He said all of this while he was under oath in a court room. It couldn't have been further from the truth. Everything he said was a downright lie.

I just shared a brief history of my life with you so you can see where I came from, see what I've been through, and see that I didn't give up despite the challenges that I've had to overcome. Throughout the majority of my life I've been dead broke just like 98% of the world's population. That's why I'm the best person for you to learn from when it comes to getting rich from home. In this book, I'm going to teach you exactly how one single idea changed my life forever, all within forty-eight hours. If you'll study and take action on the information that I share with you, I promise you that your life can also change for the better within the next forty-eight hours. If you're ready to get rich, pay off all your debt, and start living the life of your dreams, let's get started!

Chapter Two:

Business Ownership

I always tell people that numbers never lie. It doesn't matter whether you're white or black, young or old, male or female, or where you live in the world, two plus two is four. This will never change because numbers don't lie. This chapter is about FACTS! Facts about being a Business Owner compared to being an employee. You cannot argue with what I'm about to share with you because these are the FACTS. I decided to write a chapter about the facts so you can see how valuable what I'm going to share with you really is. So, open your mind to what I'm about to share with you because it may go against everything you've been brainwashed to believe your entire life. What you're about to learn might make you upset, or make you feel like you've been betrayed your entire life by the lies the world has told you. The world that we live in is very corrupt. There's a few select families in the world that control absolutely everything. These families want you to stay poor so that they can become even richer. Well, I'm going to teach you the truth so that you can become rich too.

Fact #1: Business Owners make more money than employees.

Fact #2: Business Owners get huge tax benefits from the government, but employees don't.

Fact #3: Business Owners can make unlimited income, but employees can't.

Fact #4: Business Owners get looked at as authority figures in the world, but employees don't.

Fact #5: Business Owners can work as little as they want, but employees can't.

Fact #6: Business Owners can give themselves a raise anytime they want, but employees can't.

Fact #7: Business Owners have more freedom than employees do.

Fact #8: Business Owners can be by the side of someone they love in an emergency, but employees can't.

So, as you can see, it is tremendously beneficial to become a Business Owner, if you're not already. The facts prove it. However, did you know that only 2% of the world's population own their own business? That to me is very sad. That's why 98% of the world is dead broke. It's impossible to get rich working at a job for someone else. Throughout this book, I'm going to encourage you greatly to start your own business. Until you do, you will never get rich. You need to be in control of your income and that's not possible as an employee.

However, put your fears aside. Becoming a Business Owner is nothing what you think it is. You don't need to have a college degree. You don't need to have the brains of Bill Gates. You don't need a lot of money. You don't need a lot of time. The ONLY thing you need to become a Business Owner is a burning desire to change your life. You'll learn as you go just like I have.

Remember what the title of my book says? It's true! I changed my life on a part time basis with only $20. I'm going to teach you how to do the same exact thing. All you have to do is be 100% teachable by following the steps that I teach. What's even better for you is that I'm specifically going to teach you how to get rich with a Home-Based Business. So, you don't ever have to worry about managing employees, paying expensive monthly rent for a storefront, keeping track of payroll, commuting to an office building every single day, answering phone calls, meeting with clients in person over coffee, or any of the headaches that come with traditional business ownership. Owning a Home-Based Business is the easiest and fastest way to get rich in the world today.

Let me first share with you some different businesses that I encourage you NOT to get involved in. These businesses will end up costing you a lot of time and money. Not to mention that 99% of people who start these kinds of businesses never make a single penny. I don't want you to waste ten years of your life, or $100,000 trying to get rich like I did. I know you want to get rich fast and I totally understand your urgency. I support your eagerness 100%. Stay away from the following so-called businesses:

1. **Stuffing Envelopes**. Yes, I fell for this. This is the biggest lie out there. Stay away from this get rich quick scheme. You'll only waste your time and money just like I did.

2. **Buying A Real Estate Package**. A person can definitely get rich from investing in real estate. However, you do not need to waste $50,000 going to a real estate seminar for a week. Yes, this is actually out there and people are falling for it every day. My advice for getting rich in real estate is

simple. Buy a property for $20,000 and sell it for $50,000. Duh, it doesn't take a week long seminar to learn that. Real estate is common sense, but unfortunately, common sense isn't common at all any more.

3. **Investing In The Stock Market**. In my opinion this is one of the riskiest things you could ever do. Why? Because you have no control over your money. I would rather take a chance playing Russian roulette than to give all my money to a stranger.

4. **Buying Bitcoin**. This seems to be the newest scam going around in the world. And yes, millions of people are falling for it. It's a very secretive thing that is getting people thrown in prison. Definitely not worth it.

Chapter Three:

Tax Benefits

One of the many reasons why you must become a Business Owner if you want to get rich is because of the amazing Tax Benefits that you'll receive from the government. The government rewards Business Owners with huge savings on their taxes because they're stimulating the economy with growth. Employees don't stimulate the economy, so that's why they get robbed on their taxes. Let me build even more value for you to start your own Home Based Business by explaining how much money you'll save every year on your taxes.

There is no such thing as job security anymore, and even if there was, you would still be securely broke. It's impossible to get rich working at a job. Don't ever forget that. The people in the world who are rich are Business Owners. Most people only think that Business Owners are rich because they make more mcney than employees do, but that's not the only reason. A big reason why Business Owners get rich compared to employees is because of all the tax deductions they receive.

The average employee pays 35% or more of their earnings to the government in taxes. Well, I know some Business Owners that only pay 5-10% of their earnings in taxes. They do this legally! Everyday expenses that employees have to spend money on Business Owners can write off as tax deductions. Let me give you an example so you can see what I mean.

Just in case you don't know what a tax deduction is, let me explain that to you first:

Tax deduction: something that helps you save money on your taxes at the end of the year. A tax deduction has a cash value when it comes time to file your taxes.

In America, we pay taxes on what is called the Adjusted Gross Income. This is the money you make minus the deductions you legally qualify for. Let's use Bob as an example. Bob earns $50,000 per year at his current job. As an employee, he would pay taxes on all of the $50,000. However, as a Business Owner, let's say Bob also earns $50,000 per year, but he qualifies for $10,000 in deductions. This means that Bob would only have to pay taxes on $40,000. If Bob is in the 25% tax bracket then this means he saved $2,500 in taxes. Not bad huh? I don't know about you, but an extra $2,500 that stays in my pocket is much better than if I had to give it to the government. As they say, a penny saved is a penny earned. In order to get rich, it isn't about how much money you make. It's all about how much money you keep. Being a Business Owner allows you to keep a lot more of your money.

Let me break this down for you a little bit more in detail. I'll continue to use Bob as the example. Bob made $50,000 last year at his job. He was happy during tax season last year because he received a $1,500 tax refund. However, he's not going to be happy when he finds out what I'm going to say next. You see, Bob had already paid out around $11,500 to the IRS from the money that was taken out of each of his paychecks.

So therefore, he paid $10,000 in taxes. What if Bob could get back more at the end of the year? What if he could get back closer to $10,000? Let me show you how this would be possible for Bob if he had a Home-Based Business on the side of his full time job.

Let's look at Bob's monthly expenses:
Car costs.
Eating out.
Cell phone bill.
Gas & electricity.
Mortgage payment.

As an employee, Bob doesn't get any tax deductions from these expenses. However, as a Home-Based Business Owner, a portion of these expenses would be tax deductible. Let's say that Bob's cell phone bill is $100 per month. That's a total of $1,200 per year.

Since Bob is in the 25% tax bracket, this means he would save $300 at the end of the year just from his cell phone. You get this number by taking $1,200 and multiplying it by 25%. He's spending the same amount of money on his cell phone bill each year that the rest of his coworkers spend. However, since he now owns a Home-Based Business on the side, he actually spends $300 less each year than his coworkers do. That's how the rich get richer and the poor get poorer. The rich pay less in taxes. In order to pay less in taxes you must get some tax deductions from the government. The best way to do this is to own a Home-Based Business.

Chapter Four:

Numbers Don't Lie

Did you know that 98% of America's population is dead broke?

Did you know that 98% of America's population are employees?

Did you know that only 2% of America's population is wealthy?

Did you know that only 2% of America's population are business owners?

Based on these numbers, it doesn't take a genius to figure out if you want to be wealthy in life you must be a business owner. I'm pretty sure the 98% know this, but I'm not sure why they continue to be employees. You see, numbers don't lie. Whether you're male or female, young or old, black or white, live in America or

Saudi Arabia, two plus two equals four everywhere in the world, every single day of the week. Why you ask? Because numbers don't lie. I'm going to spend some time in this chapter talking about numbers for that very reason. Once you understand the power of numbers it will teach you how to generate money, wealth, and prosperity a lot faster. Pay close attention! Let me remind you what the title of this book is:

HOW TO GET RICH FROM HOME ON A PART TIME BASIS WITH ONLY $20!

Again, I wanted to bring this to your attention for the simple fact that if you want to experience more money, wealth, and prosperity in your life, you must become a business owner, if you're not already. Not only do you have to be a business owner, but you must never take shortcuts. Trying to take a shortcut on your way to success will postpone it even longer. This book will definitely teach you about entrepreneurship, but you must be willing to act on what you learn. No one ever became successful by simply reading a book, but many people became successful doing what they learned from reading a book.

An entrepreneur is someone who will get downright sick to their stomach even thinking about what it would be like to work for someone else as an employee. Entrepreneurs are the people who make up the 2% class. For the most part, entrepreneurs are "C" students in school. They're the ones who create companies and have the "A" students work for them.

Entrepreneurs are the few people who control all the money, wealth, and prosperity in the world. They should though. Entrepreneurs are risk takers. They live their lives by faith, while everyone else lives by sight. That's why they make more money. They're willing to do things when everyone else is scared. If the world didn't have entrepreneurs the world wouldn't exist. There's so much more money for entrepreneurs than there is for employees because the competition is so much smaller.

You must remember that 98% of America's population are employees. That's a lot of people fighting for just a few jobs. However, only 2% of America's population are writing their own paychecks as business owners. Don't you think you would pay yourself more than your boss does? Then do it! Stop making excuses and start taking action!

To become an entrepreneur, you must first stop making the excuses you've made up to this point as to why you haven't been one yet. As of right now, if you're not currently a business owner, it's only because of one or more of the following excuses:

-I'm too old.

-I'm too young.

-I'm married with kids.

-I don't have the time.

-I don't have the skills.

-I don't have the money.

Well, guess what? You can make money or you can make excuses, but you can't make both. So, you're going to have to choose right now which one it's going to be? Entrepreneurs make a lot of money because they don't make any excuses.

After you read the following numbers you no longer have a right to make excuses. If you want to have a lot of money, wealth, and prosperity, you have to release all of your excuses.

Did you know that forty years old is the average age of people who start their own business?

Did you know that less than 1% of business owners came from extremely rich backgrounds?

Did you know that 70% of business owners were married when they started their first business?

Did you know that 60% of business owners had at least one child when they started their first business?

Did you know that 75% of business owners worked as employees for at least six years before they started their first business?

So, based on these facts, it doesn't matter what your age is, what your background is, whether you're married with kids, or whether you've been working as an employee your entire life up to this point. The only thing that matters is that you stop making excuses and start your own business right now.

You now know that only 2% of the population in the United States is made up of entrepreneurs. This should get you excited. This is awesome news! This just goes to show you how unlimited the opportunities are in America. Only 2% of the entire country are entrepreneurs. Everyone else is fighting for a dead end job. No wonder the unemployment rate is so high. There's too many people and not enough jobs. That means there's more money, wealth, and prosperity for the entrepreneurs, which is exactly why the rich keep getting richer and the poor keep getting poorer. Entrepreneurship is simply a choice. Those who choose to be entrepreneurs choose to be rich, while those who choose to be employees choose to be poor. What makes a person have a lot of money, wealth, and prosperity is nothing more than a choice!

Now that you know money, wealth, prosperity, and entrepreneurship are all choices, don't you think it's time for you to start making different choices? When do you think would be the best time for you to change your life? Now or later? Alright then, what are you waiting for? Become an entrepreneur right now! Here's five great reasons why you should start your own business immediately:

1. Money. Being an entrepreneur can make you a lot of money. A lot more money than you would ever be able to make as an employee.

2. Freedom. Being an entrepreneur allows you to be your own boss, call your own shots, and not have anyone tell you what to do anymore.

3. Control. Being an entrepreneur gives you control over your time and money. You decide how much time you want to work and how much money you want to make.

4. Choices. Being an entrepreneur gives you choices. You choose who you work with every day. You choose when to take a lunch break. You choose when you go on vacation.

5. Legacy. Being an entrepreneur gives you the opportunity to leave a legacy behind for your heirs.

I hope you see how amazing life can be as an entrepreneur? In my opinion, there's really no other way to live. Being an employee is the same thing as being a slave. I'll never understand why someone would voluntarily put themselves through that for fifty years. Every employee I've ever known hates their job, feels like they're overworked, feels like they're underpaid, and wastes their entire life doing something they don't enjoy. Life is too short for that. Stop making excuses and start taking action! It's time for you to become an entrepreneur right now. I'm going to teach you how I did it. Read on.

Chapter Five:

My Secret

I'm sure you're probably wondering what my secret is right? How did I get rich from home on a part time basis with only twenty dollars?

Start a Book Publishing Company! Don't worry, it's nothing what you think it is. Actually, it's ten times easier and ten times less expensive than you think it is. This is exactly what I did on a part time basis with only twenty dollars. It changed my life forever! Starting your own book publishing company is nothing more than writing a book and selling it on Amazon. Let me give you some proven statistics that will hopefully inspire and motivate you to start writing your first book immediately.

-99.75% of the world's population has had a thought at some point throughout their lives to write a book.

-However, less than 1% of the world's population have ever actually done it.

-Out of the less than 1% of people who have written a book, only six out of one thousand actually publish the book and sell a single copy.

-Out of the few published authors in the world who do write and publish a book, the average book published only sells about seventy-five copies in a lifetime.

If you make it past the four stages listed here, you are now in a very elite group of people that consists of less than 1/1000th of 1% of the world's population.

Now, hopefully these numbers don't scare you, but instead, inspire you and highly motivate you. Here's why:

It isn't hard to reach this milestone at all. You see, 99.9999% of the world's population gave up on their dream of writing a book. The reason why they gave up is because of some type of ridiculous fear that kept them from taking action. I've already become a successful published author, so all you have to do is follow my teaching.

There's only three things you need to do in order to join this elite group:

1. Sit down and write your book.

2. Submit and publish your book on Amazon.

3. Learn some marketing tips on how to generate traffic to your book.

That's it! In the first four months of 2017, I wrote, edited, published, and sold fourteen different books to people all over the world. All the statistics I just mentioned, I've already surpassed. If I can do it, so can you. The only thing keeping you from joining me as a Published Author is taking action. You have no competition because 99.9999% of the world's population will never take action. So, just by sitting down and taking action, which is writing your book, you've already succeeded. Fear is what keeps almost everyone in the world from ever getting started. Fear is nothing more than an acronym that stands for:

False Expectations Appearing Real

Think about it for a minute. Fear is nothing more than you expecting false things to appear. Let me put it into perspective for you this way. Let's say a man wants to go out with a certain woman. She's nice, sweet, caring, and absolutely beautiful. He wants to go out with her badly. He tells himself he's going to ask her out, but then when he comes face to face with her he chickens out. Why? Because he's afraid. He fears getting rejected. He tells himself that she is way too beautiful and she would never go out with a guy like him. He tells himself that she has wealthy parents and his parents are poor. He tells himself that she's perfect and he has a past like it's nobody's business. What is his problem? He's filled with fear. He's expecting things that are false. Fear is talking him out of what he wants to do. How many times have you done something like this? I've done it too. We all have, but you can't do it anymore. You can't afford to ever do it again. It's costing you too much. Do you know why it took me until I was thirty-eight years old to write my first book? FEAR. I had some false expectations that actually appeared real to me, but they weren't. I feared that my book wouldn't be any good. I feared that people would make fun of me for writing a book. I feared that people would think that I think I'm better than they are for writing a book. And most of all, I feared that no one would ever buy my book.

You see, our fears are costing us everything. By letting fear get the best of us and keeping us from taking action, we're losing out on money, new relationships, traveling the world, and living out the life of our dreams. Enough is enough. No more fear! You know something about a certain topic that a lot of people in the world don't know anything about. I'm a genius when it comes to losing weight. I'm extremely confident in saying that I know more than 99.9% of all the people in the world about losing weight. Exercise, Nutrition, and Supplementation are my specialties. It's what I've practiced and preached for well over twenty years.

Once I got over my fears, I realized millions of people want to lose weight, but simply don't know how. Well, I do know how and I also know that people would pay money to find out what I know. So, I finally put my fears to the side, I stopped making excuses, and I took massive action.

I got onto my computer, opened up Microsoft Word, and began writing everything I knew about losing weight. I knew so much for so long that the information came flying out of my heart and onto the screen in front of me. Within forty-eight hours, my book was up on Amazon for the entire world to see and purchase.

My first book that I wrote is titled:
How To Lose Weight With Intermittent Fasting

It's being sold to people all over the world on Amazon right now as a paperback book, as well as a digital download in the Kindle format. See for yourself by clicking this link:
www.amazon.com/author/fitchristophermitchell

I know you might be saying, but Christopher, I don't know how to write a book. I've never written a book before. Well, guess what? Everyone in the world can say that and most people do. That's what keeps them from ever actually doing it. However, I decided to stop making excuses and started writing a book. I didn't know anything either, but I decided to take action anyway. I learned along the way and now I can teach you how to write a book too. I've had people buy my books from many different countries all over the world. These are countries that I've never been to before in my life. If I can do it, so can you. Put your fear aside and let me help you.

Chapter Six:

My Proven Method

What if I told you that I have a proven method that you can follow that will guarantee you a published book listed on Amazon. Would you want that method? Would you use that method? Would you be forever grateful for that method? If so, keep reading and I'll share it with you.

To finish up this book and our time together, let me give you a few more reasons why you should start writing your first book immediately.

1. Writing and publishing your first book will give you instant authority and credibility. When you become a Published Author, people will see you as an expert in your field. People then value your opinion and look to you as a reliable source of information.

2. Writing and publishing your first book will give you the opportunity to change millions of people's lives all over the world. You're only one person and therefore, can only be at one place at one time. However, you can share yourself with the entire world through a published book.

3. Writing and publishing your first book will put you in front of people you never would have had a chance to get in front of before. Rich and successful people read books. If people like your book they will contact you. Some of these people might pay you a lot of money for a speaking engagement that they're in charge of. As a Published Author, you're now in a respected position where you have the ability to effect change in the world.

4. Writing and publishing your first book can give you media coverage for your work as an expert in your field. Journalists, Reporters, and Bloggers are always looking for credible people to provide valuable information to their audience. When you have media coverage circulating around you as a Published Author, it can lead to lucrative publicity for you as you're wanted to do interviews and getting featured in articles.

5. Writing and publishing your first book can attract new clients to you, resulting in more money. When you become a Published Author, people will want to do business with you and new business opportunities can come your way that previously would have been unavailable to you.

6. Writing and publishing your first book can build your business, or give

you the opportunity to start a business. As a Published Author, your book can now be used as a marketing tool to sell your other products and services. Your book enhances your reputation and gives you more value in the marketplace.

7. Writing and publishing your first book will give you another stream of income. A stream of residual income I might add. That's the best kind of income in the world. Imagine publishing a book just one time, but five years later, you're still receiving paychecks for that book.

I hope you see the value in becoming a Published Author. Doors will open for you that never would have opened for you otherwise. Every single time you write a book you give yourself a raise. Being a Published Author can make you a lot of money.

As promised, I'm now going to share my proven method with you. My proven method will absolutely guarantee that you will have a published book listed on Amazon. Just do what I share with you. Follow my teaching and your book will be right beside mine on Amazon.

My second book that I wrote is titled: **SELL YOUR FIRST BOOK!** This book teaches you my exact, step by step process of how you can Write, Edit, Publish, and Sell your very first book on Amazon within forty-eight hours from right now. This is my number one best-selling book. This book is a must have if you want to become a Published Author. Since I didn't have anyone teach me how to properly write, edit, publish, and sell my first book, I decided to give other first time authors an exact, step by step blueprint to follow so they can't fail when it comes time for them to write their first book. Get my book titled **SELL YOUR FIRST BOOK!** and everything I shared with you in this book can manifest for you. You can get the book on Amazon here: www.amazon.com/author/fitchristophermitchell

SELL YOUR FIRST BOOK! will teach you absolutely everything you need to do in order to become a Published Author. If you do exactly what it teaches you could have your own book selling to people all over the world on Amazon in as little as forty-eight hours from right now. I know this to be true because every single book I write and publish I do in less than forty-eight hours. Contact me when you publish your first book. I'll be the first person to buy it and write you a five star customer review. I wish you the best!

Personal message from the author: Thank you for getting this book. This book is simply an introduction to me as an author and a way for you to learn how to start a business if you're currently an employee.

If you've never been an Entrepreneur before, let me teach you something here. An Entrepreneur is someone who refuses to work for someone else. An Entrepreneur is someone who wants to be in control of every area of his or her life. A serious Entrepreneur will work harder than any employee ever will. Once you become an Entrepreneur, you will never work at a job for someone else again. An Entrepreneur also believes in having many different sources of income, while an employee believes in having only one source of income. This is why it's impossible for an employee to get rich.

I shared that with you to say this. I don't just make all my money from my books. Yes, I absolutely make money (residual income) from my books, but that's not my only source of income. I have several different sources of income. My best sources of income is my home-based business with ACN, my book sales on Amazon, and my real estate properties.

If you want to get paid every month when people around the world pay their tv, gas, electric, internet, and cell phone bills, you're welcome to join my team in ACN. I'll become your personal mentor and teach you how to succeed. If you'd like to get more information on the ACN opportunity, watch the video on my website here: www.ChangeYourLifeOvernight.com

If you enjoyed reading this book, here's more books by the author:

-Sell Your First Book

-Vision Board Success

-Faith Produces Miracles

-My Inspiring True-Life Story

-Money Meditation Manifestation

-Why You're Fat & Sick And How To Fix It

-How To Lose Weight With Intermittent Fasting

-How To Make Money As An Author Selling Your Books On Amazon

-Network Marketing Success, Failure, & Everything In Between

All books can be purchased from:
www.amazon.com/author/fitchristophermitchell